Writing on Your Feet

FRANK CATALANO

ISBN-13: 9780692241028
ISBN-10: 0692241027

Lexington Avenue Press
www.lexingtonavepress.com

818-994-2779

BOOKS BY FRANK CATALANO

Art of the Monologue
Monologues they haven't heard yet

The Creative Audience
The collaborative role of the audience in the creation of the visual and performing arts

White Knight Black Night
Short monologues for auditions

The Resting Place
a play

Autumn Sweet
a play

Rand Unwrapped
Confessions of a Robotech Warrior

Che Che
A screenplay

Short Monologues for Auditions

WRITING ON YOUR FEET – **Improvisational Techniques for Writers** was first presented as part of the 25th Annual Writer's Conference sponsored by San Diego State University on February 6 through the 8th, 2009 at the Double Tree Hilton Hotel in Mission Hills, California. The following transcript was presented and recorded by Frank Catalano as part of the programs offered at the conference.

Writers of fiction and non-fiction and industry professionals from the publishing business primarily attended the 25th Annual Writer's Conference. Mr. Catalano's seminars focused upon those writers seeking to adapt their novels into screenplays. The complete list of seminar presentations by Frank Catalano for this conference is:

BOOK 1:   WRITE GREAT CHARACTACTERS IN THE FIRST TEN PAGES

BOOK 2:   WRITING ON YOUR FEET - IMPROVISATIONAL TECHNIQUES FOR WRITERS

BOOK 3:   START YOUR STORY AT THE END

BOOK 4:   THE FIRST TEN PAGES

BOOK 5:   BOOK TO SCREEN

BOOK 6:   ACTING IT OUT – IMPROVISATIOINAL TECHNIQUES FOR WRITERS II

BOOK 7:   WRITE GREAT DIALOGUE

TABLE OF CONTENTS

WRITING
ON
YOUR FEET
Improvisational Techniques for Writers

SAN DIEGO STATE UNIVERSITY
25th Annual Writers Conference

WORKSHOP TRANSCRIPT
HOW TO ADAPT YOUR NOVEL INTO A SCREENPLAY

BOOK 2

Frank Catalano

SEMINAR INTRODUCTION

Welcome. I am Frank Catalano and this is WRITING ON YOUR FEET. Before we begin, I will tell you a bit about me. Some of you already know me from yesterday's programs but for those whom I am meeting for the first time today, my background is in Theatre Arts. I teach at the University of Southern California for the past thirty-eight years and I am at other schools teaching acting, writing, film and television. All those kinds of things and I teach privately as well. I have also worked at various entertainment companies including Lorimar Studios, Warner Brothers (probably the longest), 20th Century Fox and many others – serving various functions in both production and distribution. All of these experiences have given me the opportunity a better understanding of the many different aspects of the entertainment industry. It is not as simple as "you have a script and then you make it into a movie or television show." As these mediums are collaborative arts, there are many other considerations. In addition, I have had the opportunity to work on many animated films and television projects. The longest animated series were ROBOTECH and DIGIMON – DIGITAL MONSTERS. I was also able to perform as an actor character voices for both of these projects.

In animation, when you write and you go in and pitch ideas; you wind up performing all of the voices within your story and sometimes, you actually do the voice of the characters. As an author, I have written several books. *I have two books out: ART OF THE MONOLOGUE (2007). It's a theatre book for actors with original monologues and a large section on monologue performance theory. I've also had plays produced and published. I have a new play being published right now and I have a brand new book coming out this month called THE CREATIVE AUDIENCE – THE COLLABORATIVE ROLE OF THE AUDIENC IN THE CREATION OF THE VISUAL AND PERFORMING ARTS (2009) and so it is not being sold in the lobby.

*Since this presentation in 2009, Frank Catalano has published the following books:

    ART OF THE MONOLOGUE (2007)
    THE CREATIVE AUDIENCE (2009)

WHITE KNIGHT BLACK NIGHT – SHORT MONOLOGUES FOR AUDITIONS (2010)

AUTUMN SWEET – A PLAY (2011)

THE RESTING PLACE – A PLAY (2011)

RAND UNWRAPPED – CONFESSIONS OF A ROBOTECH WARRIOR (2012)

CHE CHE – A SCREENPLAY (2013)

SHORT MONOLOGUES FOR AUDITIONS (2013)

MYTHS AND TANGOS (2014)

Now that you know a little bit about me, what I would like to do and this won't take long. I'd like to be able to send you additional information about our discussion here today via email. I am passing out this form and if you would like to provide your name and email addresses that would be great.

And when I send you a summary of our discussion today, you will have my email address, if you have any questions.

(Audience member asks – what if you already have their email from a previous seminar?)

Please enter it for this seminar again.

WRITING ON YOUR FEET

Today's seminar is called WRITING ON YOUR FEET and it's just a quick (you know) catchy title for utilizing improvisational techniques for writing or adaptation of your literary work (novel) into a screenplay. Many actors use improvisation to help them create characters and dialogue. However, many writers are reticent to get up out of their chairs and put their work "on its feet" because they are trained to do all of their creating mentally. This is fine. But as a writer I wanted to say that using the improvisational approach—I mean actually getting up and "doing" instead of "sitting" engages all of your senses. Why? To give you a better understanding of your story and the characters that live in the universe you have created.

Yesterday, we were having a discussion about a play that I had written. I had an offer to publish it but I hadn't read it in a very long while and wanted to look at it one more time before I was going to put it in print. Why? Because time had passed, I wanted to see if the work still did what I thought it did for an audience when I first created it. So, my way of accomplishing this was to put it up on its feet. Of course, I could have sit down in my living room and read it again – but I want to engage all of my senses. This was my answer. It worked for me.

And it can work for you as well. This putting on its feet and read aloud can assist all of us whether you are a fiction writer or a screenwriter – it serves you to experience your work on multiple levels – and be on its feet, read aloud by actors And, we're in Los Angeles (San Diego) there are so many actors that would be glad to help you do just that.

So, I decided to have a staged reading and put my play up on its feet and watch and listen to it (instead of read it.) That's what I did. And it was very helpful for me. I listened, watched, made notes and some revisions. I found it to be a short cut way of getting to the core of what the play was about and what I was trying to say to my audience. And so when we write, we engage our senses.

When you are sitting and you are writing on your laptop or perhaps a legal pad (everyone has their own method), you visualize your characters and hear their voices in your mind. Isn't that true? Have you ever heard of the Italian playwright Luigi Pirandello? Once of his most famous plays is SIX CHARACTERS IN SEARCH OF AN AUTHOR... a very good play. Pirandello had the hardest time writing because of his jealous wife. When he wrote, he would like himself in his studio to write so his wife couldn't disturb him. His way of writing was to speak his character's voices out loud and when he did, his wife (hearing voices through the locked door) was convinced that he had a woman in the studio with him. She would often pound on the door while he was trying to write. Not an easy way to write, but Pirandello believed, as a writer, that this method was an effective way of creating characters and story for his plays. What about putting your characters on their feet?

What about putting your characters on their feet with little or no written material? Some of you are thinking, "I just have an idea, nothing else but an idea. How can my characters get up and talk? They are not fully developed. How can they or I say anything? I can't do it." I say, "yes you can" and that's exactly what you are going to do today. I want to explore putting your characters on their feet and letting them talk (they could actually be sitting too – it doesn't matter). I want you to be able to listen to them, watch them move and learning. No takers? So, even if I got two of you today and I place you within an improvisational scene within your idea – you provide the idea, the characters and we will let the characters play it out? What do you think? Remember, the writer doesn't have to write down every single word his/her characters say – they may not all work. But what you can get is an understanding of your characters, how they might relate and how they move within their universe. Also, it is really helpful to improvise the same scenario (idea) several times? What happens then?

What happens is a magical little thing... truth. I don't know if you can put your finger on it but the truth (of your idea) kind of floats to the top... and what I mean by that is that the underlying meaning starts to reveal itself as it is experienced by a larger number of people. We could have fifty or sixty people in this room form groups and send them to several corners of this hotel (so they can see or hear what is happening in here). Then bring them in one group at a time and have them improvise the same exact scenario (idea). The result? There will be repetition and there will be differences in each group's improvisation. However, there will be certain qualities, themes, characteristics that will be evident in most or all. What comes out of the experiment is that the idea has a universal through line or truth that can be see in whole or part in all of the improvisations. If there is conflict within it with a certain kind of resolution and you say, "Okay, then, that's the way it will be. I'm going to incorporate that element into my idea or maybe I'm not going in the right direction. None of the improvisations reflect my idea at all."

Improvisation can be a tool that you can use to work within a framed scenario…

(Catalano hand an email list by audience member)

Thank you. … or idea to take it to the next level. When you are under a lot of pressure to write, you know you have to have the project in by a certain deadline.

WRITING USING MOVING PICTURES

During the Robotech series, the writing and production (all of it) happened all at once. There was always a looming deadline hanging over our heads. To make matters worse, the writers and the actors for that matter during the making of the show were never really totally sure of what it was about. Like the CIA, we were just given small parts to work on and never really got a sense of the whole. This was not in anyway a nefarious plot to hide some dark secret from all of us. It was just the crazy nature of how that show came together. The big picture was really only known by one person, the shows producer the late Carl Macek (1951 – 2010). Carl had a creative vision for the show as a whole and had a sense of how the story was going to play out and would summarize each episode's footage. Remember, the show was being written to already existing animated footage. What the writers wrote had to fit that footage; they couldn't just write whatever they wanted. But the challenge was, what to write within that footage and to make sure it all fit as a whole. We used to call Carl Macek "the chees master" because he could look at a small clip or a whole episode in Japanese and then spin off (with extreme detail) what was going on in that particular episode and how it all fit in to the larger mosaic. For the rest of us... not Carl people... it was Japanese anime and we had very little to go on except the visual components of what we were looking at.

To write a Robotech episode, you would start with a plot summary (there was also a show Bible) and a twenty-two minute episode that had been time coded so that you can write the dialogue and effects in sync. One way to do it was to read the summary, and then try to figure out how to get that done ahead of time as if you were writing a script for a movie. But that really (in my opinion) doesn't work because you have got to consider the footage. Remember, you are only writing the dialogue and reactions. Pretty easy... right?

Let me say, writing for anime is not for the faint hearted. You have got to be true to the characters (or the fans will fry you) and you have got to put words in the character's mouths that fit. The real challenge is to try to find words that makes sense and at the same time fit into the characters moving mouths. If it were not written "in sync" then it would have to be written correctly in the studio by the director... trust me you don't want that to happen.

A second method is to understand the framework of the story as stated in the summary. Know where you are going and where you have to end up and then let the characters tell you what they are saying. What I mean by this is essentially writing on your feet. Let the physicality of the characters determine what they say. It's a lot easier, because you are not burdened by the structure of a preexisting script. Sometimes having a script is harder than "not" having a script. Once in a while, on some shows, we would get scripts written in English directly from Tokyo and they would be literal translations like "Hey watch it man or I will beat you into many pulps!"

(Audience laughter)

Even with their script, you have no story. Well you actually have less than a story so you are better off throwing the literal translation out and let the characters do the talking. Just play the footage and start talking for the characters as they move through the frames. What happens then? At some point the story and the characters start to emerge clearly and a framework is established. The same process happens with you view a movie with subtitles. In the beginning you read every word and then after a while you begin to understand character and situation over and above what is being written in the subtitle. Now, my experience with letting my characters talk has only one problem, sometimes they sound like me and say things that maybe I would say. This happens a lot in the dubbing studio when you are working very late at night... you are tired and suddenly your not voicing what is written but instead putting in your own "very in sync" lines. During the Robotech series, my character Rand is in the middle of an Invid invasion when he rides his version of a motorcycle up to another character's mother and says something (I don't remember what was actually written) but I said, and it fit perfectly "GET A JOB." We recorded the correct line as well but somehow GET A JOB made it to the final cut and was aired as part of the show when it played on television. Of course, the Robotech fans, were not fooled for a minute and knew it was a mistake… but the fact is, the line still remains today and when I see Robotech fans, they ask me to autograph their pictures with "Get a job…"

So the immense power of writing on your feet is evident. But I will give you another example that is even sillier than GET A JOB. I was writing and co producing a series called THE ADVENTURES OF DYMAMO DUCK for FOX KID'S NETWORK. I was part of a writing team that had to convert over three hundred hours of raw animal footage based upon the French film maker Jean Tourane's idea for a children's television series *Saturnin le canard* about the duckling Saturnin who had all kinds of adventures. The series was produced using real animals, dressed up with sunglasses, hats and other props that lived inside a miniature world. A small duck was the main character, fighting crimes of the evil Dr. Mortek (a monkey) and other assorted villains. The animals wander around on miniature sets with scale models of trucks and other vehicles. The duck's name was changed to "Dynamo Duck."

(Audience laughter)

Remember, this was not "wild life" footage – this was a duck wearing a bow tie driving a little car and or flying a biplane. None of the animals were hurt – nothing like that. But this series was totally written on its feet!

(Audience laughter)

Basically, our first step was take all the raw animal footage and cut into smaller workable sections. We did this in a studio at my home doing what they called back then "paper cuts" and then would assemble the raw material into actual episodes. I think we did about two hundred of them. Each episode had the same reoccurring characters (ducks, gerbils, frogs, goldfishes, weasels) but each had a different stand-alone storyline. Almost all of the writing was done "on its feet" working off the visual images that were contained in the footage that was cut for each episode. There was no way we could, apart from the footage, come up with "gags" or setups with payoffs at the end as you would in a traditional script. Also, remember, we had to tell a story. There had to be a narrative structure with a beginning middle and end. My writing partner for this project, Gregory Snegoff worked for hours creating what finally became the basis for all cut footage and dialogue spoken for each episode. After we created the framework, we gave some of the episodes to other writers to complete specific "in sync" sections of dialogue. You may be wondering "How do you write "in sync" dialogue to a duck or a gerbil?" That is a seminar all into itself and Greg Snegoff is the master at putting words or sounds in the mouths of just about anything you could imagine. An example for the Dynamo Duck character, the actual duck used in the filming (there were probably several) would from time to time shake his head. We wrote actual lines every time the duck would move his mouth (no computers here) and then (no matter when) if the duck shook his head, we would insert a "sheesh" to the line. Here we are working directly off of the visual image. So the visual image is the key.

There was one episode that featured a whole group of little yellow ducklings waddling about, dressed in little pirate hats. So, we decided to use the footage we had and do a pirate story. We cut the footage and wrote a short summary of the storyline that should go with it. All a scriptwriter had to do was write dialogue. The writer who was assigned came back a few days later and said, "I can't do this anymore!"

(Audience laughter)

"I don't know what to write? I've used my three pirate jokes and now I don't know what else I could write for them to say?" My reply? Stop thinking in terms of literal narrative (duck jokes or pirate jokes) (he was in fact an excellent writer) with a setup and pay off. Just watch the footage and let it lead you to a situation and the rest will take care of itself. Writing on your feet is a moment-to-moment kind of a thing. That's the best approach to this sort of writing. Because he had written the same way all his life, he just couldn't grasp it and many writers approach their work in the same manner.

And so my point is, sometimes we have this overall concept of something we want to tell and we can't do it because we are locked into the idea itself and don't know where to start. How many times have we had the blank page and no matter what we right we say to ourselves over and over again…"no that's no good" "no that's not right…" Instead, think about just taking it moment to moment. It could be a simple little thing we you start with a situation where two characters come into a space. And that's all you've got to start with. The say, "Hi how are you?" Your two characters are on a bus stop and one of them is a CIA agent. Then, Go! And all of a sudden the two begin to connect and react to one another in that simple space. One speaks, then the other back and forth back and forth. Now, out of that exchange a couple of things can happen.

One, it totally dissolves into "nothing." That's part of being an artist. Two, it can begin to formalize and become something else. It flowers. But it becomes something totally different. Your CIA agent and the person they meet by chance at a bus stop fall in love. And now all of a sudden, it's a love story. And you go, "Whoa, okay? I'll take that." Then you start building it from there.

WRITING USING YOUR FIVE SENSES

So, when we get up and start moving our characters, it gives us some opportunities. Number one, we can listen to them engaging our sense of hearing. Now, every one of us has a different sensory order. We all have five senses, but some of our senses are stronger for us, than others. How many of you think that? How many of you think that your senses are not equal?

(Audience reacts.)

So I would personally say that I am more of a "visual" person than a listener. So, I might remember what you look like but I may not remember your name. I can say that I am visually oriented. Second place for me would be "touch." So I like to touch things a lot when I shop… and after that maybe "smell." Listening for me is probably on the bottom of the list. My wife often says to me, "You know you never listen to a word I say!" and I respond, "What?"

(Audience laughter)

Now I know you are going to say that's a guy thing. Maybe and maybe not and sometimes you can create characters that are of different sensory centers. For example, a female character tells her male lover, "You never tell me you love me." And the guy responds, "What are you talking about? I washed your car yesterday!" So she's saying I want to "hear" you "I'm auditory" while he's thinking, "I'm visual baby; here's your car, I cleaned it. I could have been watching TV."

How many have heard this? The male character says to his female lover, "I love you so much!" and she snaps back at him "Don't tell me you love me... show me... stop drinking with your buds every night."

It can work both ways. When we put our characters on their feet, we are engaging all of our senses instead of just doing it all in our head. We are engaging auditory, touch, maybe smell... let me ask you this... in your own universe, and do certain places have specific smells attached to them? And don't those individual smell sometimes evoke certain emotions or memories for you?

(Audience member, "Oh, yeah... yeah.")

I used to live in Hawaii (there's a certain floral smell there) and I'm not talking about people working at the lei stands waiting for you when you get off the plane. No not that... Hawaii has a certain smell to it (like gardenias) that is unique and I could be walking at the mall in Los Angeles – somebody will walk by and they are wearing a gardenia type of perfume and it takes me right back to Hawaii. New York has a smell too... actually more than a couple of smells.

(Audience laughter)

and some of them...

(Audience laughter – audience member comment)

There is a smell in New York which I will never forget smelling as a child when my father drove over the Kosciuszko Bridge which was a truss bridge connecting New York City's boroughs of Brooklyn and Queens. When we drove over it the smell was something like rotten eggs mixed with a dead animal. It was horrible. My dad told me that there was a meat processing plant there and that's why it smelled so bad. And now as an adult, when I smell something even remotely like that I am right back there, a child again in the back of my dad's car, going over the Kosciuszko Bridge!

(Audience laughter)

So, smell does have a way… not that I'm saying we should spray ourselves.

(Catalano acknowledges audience member)

Yes? You were going to say something… I thought you were waving at me?

(Audience laughter)

What about auditory? We hear our characters… and what about touch? We watch how our characters respond physically to one another… we watch how they touch one another. We can also experience a visual picture as two characters relate physically that tells us the story. If two characters enter a space and you are writing them, let's use our example of the CIA agent and at the bus stop.

(Catalano approaches an audience member to illustrate)

(Audience laughter)

Don't worry… I won't actually touch you.

(Audience member laughs)

I am playing your role and I sit down and I do this…

(Catalano assumes a specific physicality – sits very close but doesn't touch.)

And you go, "Wait I've never thought of this. The CIA agent, ever so slightly, touches her. What does this mean? That's for you to fill in with dialogue and narrative.

Forget about writing it… all you have to do is observe what is around you… that's what actors do. Why was I sitting so close? Maybe, I was passing a small data chip to her… or maybe, I am trying to assassinate her. Let the characters on their feet create the visual picture and physicality while you fill in the rest with dialogue. And by the way, this is not fiction… this is real.

I sat on a crowded train once in New York and there was a guy reading a newspaper standing very close to me as the train moved.

(Catalano stands close to an audience member but doesn't touch them.)

He was like this.

(Catalano stands very close to the audience member but doesn't touch him)

While he never actually touched me, which was pretty hard to do since the moving train was tossing us back and forth, he was able to get close enough to smell me. I thought I smelled okay for that time of day.

(Audience laughter)

But he reeked to stale cigarettes smoke and mothballs. Not a very fragrant combination. We were so close to each other that you could barely put a sheet of paper between us. And yet, we did not speak or acknowledge on another. One could argue that the universe that they move within governs the distance between two people on a crowded train. That is... the train is crowded and so complete strangers exist, not acknowledging one another at all even though they are less than one inch apart. Maybe because they are so close, they can smell one another. One reeks of stale cigarettes and beer; the other of cheap cologne. What does that say about each character and how can you explain this? It can only be explained by the nature of the physical universe they live in. Now take this same scenario and move it to a place like Los Angeles. I was on line and a supermarket and I'm waiting on line and some guy is behind me... the check out person was moving **very slowly.**

(Catalano motions the check out person – audience laughter)

You know, one of those things. And the guy standing behind me has moved right up against me trying to make the line go faster. And the way he decided he was going to do that was to move up real close breathe down my neck and brush up against my butt. He did it once, then again and then a third time when I finally turned around and looked at him: "Don't touch my butt! It's not going to make the check out person move any faster." I felt that he was invading my space because in Los Angeles, where we are in our cars all the time and not closely packed together in trains – the amount of personal space we assume is much larger. If this same person were that close to me on a crowded train, maybe it would have been appropriate. So this is all part of writing on your feet.

All of this comes into play when you write this way. This heightened feedback and not all of it is going to be useable. Some of it is not going to work for your story. So, this method is going to tell you what to leave out as well. It is merely an experimental exploration that will provide to you a multitude of choices. You may say to yourself, "I like this, let's see where it takes me." Or "I don't like this so I will not go in that direction." It's a wonderful way to start your adaptation to a screenplay or your book. Take two characters or even one character and place them in a situation (the who, what, when and where) and then see what they do. Let the characters and the universe you have created for them take you on a journey. In a moment, we are going to try a few of these.

MANIPULATION VERSUS SELECTION

You can, as a writer, participate within an improvisation. But many of you sitting here today probably don't want to do that. You say to yourself, "I don't want to get up, I am not an actor." Or "I don't want to improvise my idea to a room full of writers." This is not a problem. If you are shy and you don't like getting on your feet, get actors to do it for you. If you don't want to share your idea, you can start your story from scratch or you can define a specific who, what, where or when. So if I said to you I have absolutely no idea about what I want to write about. I have no story. I have no characters... in short, I have nothing. But, I'm going to get two people and put them somewhere and create their physicality and maybe the universe they inhabit and start them off with just a word. Not even an important word... just a word... maybe something like "rosebud." That's it. I start the improvisation with that and from that starting point you go. You might have on your first page "CIA agent walks up to a bus stop and sits down next to a woman carrying a small leather bag close to her, like a rare book. He sits down very close to her (just like we have done today) and just says one word, "rosebud." You may wonder what does that mean? You don't have to know. Once the characters begin reacting to one another the meaning of "rosebud" begins to emerge. Then, you try the same setup with two different people and experience that situation as it evolves. There may be similar qualities or the situation may go in an entirely different direction. As the writer or creator, you use a process of selection rather than mental manipulation. What am I saying here? What is manipulation?

In writing, the process of manipulation is when the writer creates all of the details of any given situation. Every detail of what happens is written in and every outcome is carefully controlled. Then what of selection?

The writer creates a framework to develop the idea and through experimentation "selects" from what what organically evolves what will become the permanent story.

This method has its pitfalls. A lot of your experimentation may result in failure. It may also take your story and characters in a direction that was not intended. But it will also take you on a journey where you can discover elements of story and character that (although inside of you) that you would have utilized. The skill of selection is to take what you can from your experimentation that works and discard those elements that don't. But it is not wasted – you also learn from what does not work. This is writing on your feet.

WRITING USING IMPROVISATION

I was going to do what I call "TAG SCENES" Let me tell you what a "TAG SCENE" is so that you can use this technique on your own. A "TAG SCENE" is this... okay lets' try one so you can see what I'm talking about. Okay, everybody, let's get up... you need a group maybe five or ten people, put them in a circle. Let's make the circle a bit larger so we have lots of space to move. We start with just a circle.

> (Catalano selects an audience member as a volunteer and both
> move to the center of the circle.)

Let's start with you and I. I will start the improvisation and you will respond. I speak and then you speak... and we move and as the scenario develops at some point one of you (indicating audience members) will say, "FREEZE." The two people in the middle of the circle literally freeze what ever they are doing. Their physicality and speech becomes literally frozen as if they were mannequins in a store window. Then the person who stated "freeze" will come into the center of the circle and "tag" on of the two people out – then assume the exact physical stance and gesture they were in. The person tagged returns to the outer circle and can come back in again at any time What happens then, is that person, who comes in, assuming the physical gesture, breaks it and begins a whole new improvisation with a whole new who, what when and where. A totally new situation is created with a different physicality and characters until they are "frozen" by one of you. Then the improvisation ends and a new one is created by the person coming in. The entire process continues over and over again. New characters, new situations created in an endless loop. Pretty crazy eh? A couple of things to remember:

The two people in the center of the circle must be able to create a specific who, what, when and where before they are tagged out. This means, that one person can come in and say one line then gets tagged out. We have to allow them to create the basics.

When the incoming person creates a certain reality, the person already in the circle must accept it. This means if one person comes in and tags someone out, then says (as part of the new scene) "Can you press the thirteen floor for me please." And the person that already in the circles responds with "What do you mean, thirteenth floor? We are at the beach!" This would create a disconnect and the scene would be hard to create because the participants were not listening to on another.

A word about "physicality." When the person comes in and tags someone out, they must create their situation out of the physical gesture (from the person they tagged out) they have assumed. They should not, assume it then drop it and say their first line. The first line has to evolve out of the physical gesture.

Okay? Should we try a few of these?

(Nervous Audience laughter.)

I'll start. Let me say one more thing to you.

(Catalano directs his comments to the audience member with him in the middle of the circle.)

It's important that you and I are a bit "over physical." Meaning we should use larger gestures to provide specific gestures to assume for the people tagging us out and starting a new improvisation. Okay, should we try it?

(Audience member Yes!)

Okay, don't leave me up here… one of you guys has to tag me out. Okay?

(Audience member "We will tag you out after like twenty five minutes" More audience laughter.)

You can tag me out or anyone else. It doesn't matter. All of that... okay, here we go.

Oh wait a minute.

(A new person (female), not in the seminar, enters the room.)

Hi.

(Person "I feel like I'm literally walking in on writing on your feet. Did I just hear you say that I can come in?"

I did. Why don't you watch this for a second and then join us?

(Person responds, "Okay..."

Have you ever done improvisation?

(Person responds: "Oh... I hate it... but I'll watch.)

Improvisation for writers... it just clears the house out.

(Audience laughter.)

Okay, here we go – one, two, three...

(Improvisation begins Audience #1 is female)

Catalano:	"I'm really sorry I'm late honey...
Audience #1:	"I fixed your favorite meal... you always have an excuse."
Catalano:	"I had to work at the office... look I mean I've got a microphone."
Audience #1:	"You always have to work..."
Catalano:	"I know..."
Audience #1:	"I have a three year old – you want to change that!"
Catalano:	"Hi Freddie..."
Audience #1:	"God damn it!"

Catalano: "I'm sorry, look... I know I smell of perfume but it's not what you think. I was... you didn't know that did you?"

Audience #2:   "Freeze!"

Audience #1:   You... (Crying)

(Audience laughter. Then a new audience member enters and creates and entirely new scene. Catalano exits improvisation.)

Catalano: Thank you... perfect...

(Audience #1 is female and Audience #2 is male.)

Audience #2:   The aircraft looked like this... it rolled, it came on full throttle and I fired a missile down on it... it missed. It went for a roll down here... and what should I have done next?

Audience #1:   "Then what the fuck were you doing over in Israel?"

(Audience laughter)

Audience #2:   "I was fighting Arabs what else do you think I was doing over Israel?"

Audience #1:   "Did you not see the sign on the plane? It was not the Arabs you hit!"

Audience #2:   "I wasn't..."

Catalano: "Freeze..."

Excellent... excellent. I don't know if you noticed what he did? He took the physical space exactly and he made it into something else. That normally takes a long time for people to get and he just got it right out of the box. That's exactly right. Let's continue.

(Improvisation begins. Audience #1 and Audience #2 are both female.)

Audience #1:	(crying) "You told me you wouldn't tell them… you lied…"
Audience #2:	"I'm sorry… but you know I had to… it was my job. I'm a counselor and I had to tell the authorities."
Audience #1:	"Now, they're going to lock me up… (crying.)
Audience #2:	"They won't… they'll just give you counseling."
Audience #1:	(more crying)
Catalano:	"Freeze…"

(Catalano tags out one person and brings in another member of the audience.)

Catalano:	"Anyone you want… "
Audience #1:	"I'll take her."
Catalano:	"Excellent work."

(Audience #1 is male and Audience #2 is female.)

Audience #1:	"So, when I talked to Miss Suliman, I said that I thought it was actually nine embryos not just eight. So I don't know what happened. So, what am I supposed to tell the press?"
Audience #2:	"Well, first of all… you need to learn how to count. This very important Yuk Yuk Yuk – how did you pass medical school?"
Audience #1:	"Well, this wasn't my first language. You know this… I don't know what I'm going do though because the press is hounding me for more and more information and they think that I'm a creep because I put all these embryos in there…"

(Catalano cuts in.)

Catalano:	"Freeze…"

(Brings in a new audience member to tag someone out.)

Catalano: "Anyone you want."

(A new improvisation is started Audience #1 is a male and Audience #2 is a female.)

Audience #1:   "What did you expect I would think when you come in wearing... fishnet hose and a short skirt?"

Audience #2:   "I'm sorry honey, I didn't think you would notice. Didn't you realize where the extra money was coming from? It's not my fault! You know! I mean I'm paying for all your fancy cars – I had to get the money somewhere.

Audience #1:   "I'm not complaining about the money or even where it came from... but you didn't tell me. I can't pass on it... the right amount of funds to our agent – he has to know where our source of supply comes from otherwise he might complain about the wrong ten percent.

Audience #2:   "You can't tell him... you can't tell him... tell him that I'm working on the wrong side of the street!"

(Catalano ends the improvisation.)

Catalano: "...and freeze."
Good, let's make a circle... will you join us?

(Audience member reluctantly joins the group.)

(Audience laughter.)

YOU DON'T HAVE TO BE FUNNY
TO IMPROVISE

Now there's something I want to say about improvisation, I don't really need to say it here, but sometimes people participating, tell me if you think it's true, that they feel they have to be funny when they come up here. What you do and say always has to be funny?

(Several audience members indicate agreement.)

Well, it doesn't. So, you can have some real moments up here... not everything is a Saturday Night Live skit... we can also do drama. We will be doing some longer form sitting down in a minute. Now, I want to just try something – it doesn't have to be funny – it can be just real. Especially, if you are working on a dramatic piece. But dramatic pieces can also have humor in them too.

How many of you had difficulty coming up with the first line when you entered the improvisations today?

(Many of the audience members raise their hands in agreement.)

Okay, I'm going to fix that right now. I want everyone to think of a first line and make it so that it is something you can remember.

(Catalano welcomes the new member of the audience who has finally stepped into the group.)

By the way, I'm Frank Catalano.

(Audience member: "I'm Maggie.)

Hi Maggie.How do you do? Okay, here we go… okay, so what's your first line?

Audience:	"What are you doing here?"
Audience:	"Why did you kill my child?"
Audience:	"But I always wanted to do that."
Audience:	"Hello, Frankie angel…"
Audience:	"I don't want to do much of anything."

Okay, that's a good start… should I have a first line too? Here's mine

Catalano:	"I'll take cherry vanilla."

I hope I don't forget that… I know I will.

Alright, let's spread out a bit and let's start with two people in the center and we will start the first line of the improvisation with the line you have selected and the person already in the circle will respond with their first line Every time someone is tagged out, the new person coming in will always start (no matter what the physicality of the position they are taking) with the line they have selected. You know the ones we said when we went around the circle a moment ago.

Let's give a try:

(Two audience members take the center of the circle and begin)

(Note they will always be identified as Audience #1 and Audience #2.)

Audience #1:	"Hello, Frankie Angel…"
Audience #2:	"What are you doing here?"
Audience #1:	"Well, just… oh wait you weren't Frankie Angel. I'm so sorry, my bad… well I guess I better go now."

Audience #2:	"You obviously don't know what the hell you're doing here?"
Audience #1:	"Well… actually I don't. You know… Well my "meds" I thought I was going to be on certain "meds" and they got them mixed up and now I'm… I think I'm lost."
Audience #2:	"You're lost? I've got some "meds" here if you need them."

Okay cut. Good.

> (One audience member remains and one steps out of the center
> of the circle and is replaced by a different audience member.)

Come on in… remember you start with your first line and you respond with your first line.

Audience #1:	(whisper) Why did you kill my child?"
Audience #2:	"Hello, Frankie Angel…"
Audience #1:	"You're caught…"
Audience #2:	"I'm who?"
Audience #1:	"You're caught… I died to come after you."
Audience #2:	"What?"
Audience #1:	"I want to know **why** you killed my child."
Audience #2:	"I don't think I know… oh my goodness, that was your child? I thought that was my child. I'm confused, that was your child?"
Audience #1:	"I gave birth to him…"
Audience #2:	"Wait… that was **our** child… why are you saying it's your child. It's always about your child… it's always about your needs. What about **my** needs?"
Audience #1:	"I gave birth to him… I have the sagging breasts… I have the cesarean scar to prove it!"
Audience #2:	"You know what? Prove it!"

And cut… that was good. That was great!

> (Audience laughter)

Should we write that down? That was good. Oaky, let's go back out… are you okay with this?

(Audience member responds with a "yes."

I thought you said you didn't like improvisation. You know what this is… she's a "plant" who knows how to do this cold. She is going to just come in

(Audience laughter.)

and says to herself "I'm just going to play this fool…" Okay, you have your first line. Let's do another one.

Audience #1:	"I never want to do much of anything."
Audience #2:	"But I always wanted to do this…"
Audience #1:	"But I don't…"
Audience #2:	"But I do… and I thought…"
Audience #1:	"Oh, please…"
Audience #2:	"But it's really fun… it's really fun… it's great… it's great."
Audience #1:	"It could be…"
Audience #2:	"…and that parachute on the back… ignore the bricks… they put bricks in the special back packs. But's it's okay; you're going to love this. They're going to put you in a plane. It will be fabulous – you signed the insurance policy. Right?"
Audience #1:	"Sure… whatever. Just somebody is going to have to push me… because I'm not going otherwise."
Audience #2:	"They'll push you… they'll push you. I'll push you."

And cut. Good… very Hitchcock…

(Audience laughter.)

Let's bring in a new person and a new line.

(Audience member leaves and a different one comes into the circle.)

You start.

Audience #1:	"I don't want to do much of anything."
Audience #2:	"What are you doing here?"
Audience #1:	"I just walked in by mistake and it was a mistake but I didn't realize you guys would ask me to do anything."

(Audience laughter)

Audience #2:	"You mean you walked through a door that says "ACTION IN HERE" and you expected no action?
Audience #1:	"It didn't say that. It didn't say anything like that."
Audience #2:	"Did you read the door?"
Audience #1:	"No…"
Audience #2:	"Oh come on… it's on the door – I wrote it there…"
Audience #1:	"You did?"
Audience #2:	"Yes, I wrote there… I took my pen and I wrote it there."

And cut… good! Don't run away.

(Audience laughter.)

Okay, who do I want to pair up? Okay… you start.

Audience #1:	"What are you doing here?"
Catalano:	"I'd like a cherry vanilla…"
Audience #1:	"A cherry vanilla?"
Catalano:	"Yes, sir."
Audience #1:	"I'm sorry, we don't have cherry vanilla."
Catalano:	"Oh? I saw cherry over there and vanilla over here and I thought maybe you could put them together."
Audience #1:	"If you saw an elephant over there and a zebra over there would you put them together?"
Catalano:	"Look, my kid's in the car… can you give me a break? He's crying and the kid gives me… you know I really shouldn't even be here. I took…"
Audience #1:	"Look, all I have here Pee Boo Bear and Black Walnut… would you like a shake?"

Catalano:	"No, you know I took my kid… I'm not supposed to have him. My wife doesn't even know I have him and he's very upset… if you could just help me out."
Audience #1:	"Okay… is he allergic to nuts?"
Catalano:	"You know, I don't know… just give me a little cherry… I tell you what… give me two cones… one cherry and one vanilla and I'll put them together myself. Okay?"
Audience #1:	"All right, I've got some cherry here… and how about a vanilla bean?"
Catalano:	"Great… how much is that… here… I'll give you twenty bucks."
Audience #1:	"Twenty bucks… sure!"
Catalano:	"Thanks a lot."
Audience #1:	"Sure you don't want any walnut?"
Catalano:	"No, listen I gotta go… I gotta go."

Improvisation ends.

And so on… what you can see is, that you can have comedy, you can make what is said into something else. You don't have to be literal. The "Hello Frankie Angel" line does not always have to be comic. It also depends on what is added to by the other actor. You can use dialogue totally against the literal meaning or character. You can give them any meaning you want them to have within the reality of the scene. There could be an assassin and this character could be a stand up comedian. I mean it could be that kind of a thing. It doesn't always have to be literal. It's not like playing the piano where the dark lower notes are here and the higher notes are here… you can mix these elements to create your characters and story. You have to remain open and let the improvisation take you to wherever it takes you. Okay, let's try something else. Let's all sit down… you can rest now. And what I would like to do is create a scenario…

(Catalano is signaled from the back of the room.)

How am doing?

(Voice from back of room "You have got about fifteen minutes.")

FINDING THE METAPHOR – HOW NOT TO BE LITERAL

Okay. I want to create a scenario where there is nothing and try one or two with there is an actual framework given… like a break up or something like that where you can actually work within a narrative framework. But I want to try this exercise first because it will be fun… and you can sit down on this one, which will be great. Right?

(Audience laughter.)

This is not a "tag" scene and I will need two volunteers. Great! Thank you.

(Catalano pulls two people from the audience.)

(Audience laughter)

You are so kind. Great. Frankie Angel, I knew I could count on you. That's such a great opening line. Please come and sit down. So what we are trying to do here, if we may, and again what we are about to do is a "conceit" a bit of a trick. Let's say you are sitting in front of a blank page and you have absolutely "zip." What if we just had two characters, just like the two people sitting here today… and we have nothing but a blank page? What I want to do is start with a single word which one of you sitting here will say and one of you in the audience will give me in a minute. The word we start with will be a random word that the audience will give us.

Now before we begin, let me remind you (we are kind of there already) that whatever the word is, we do not have to stick to the literal meaning of that word. The word could mean something else entirely. For example, if we started with the word "brick," the entire scene would not have to be about construction materials. A "brick" could mean anything... what are some things a brick could mean?

(Audience members speak.)

"Something heavy."
 "Bulky"
 "A person's name."
 "A blockage of some sort."
 "A part of something."

All possible. So I don't want you to get tied into being literal. Use your imagination and see where the word you start with takes you and remember, don't go crazy trying to think of something funny. Just be in the moment. So, if we start with a word like "anchovies" the scene doesn't have to be about fish. The word could mean anything... it could act as a metaphor for your life. So, you can take it to another level or in some cases you might want to use the literal.

(Audience member: "How you hear it."

How you hear it... the way it is spoken... the context it is given within a scene. Now for our exercise, we are going to start you with a single word. All I want you to do is say that word and you will respond. Don't add any other word to what you say. Don't say, "Anchovies, I hate that restaurant." Just start with the word and don't try to define it. Let it define itself through the exchange of dialogue. Allow your partner to hear the word and then respond and then you respond to that line and so forth. The meaning and direction of the scene will happen on its own. It's a give and take kind of a feel. Now, I'm not going to let this scene go on forever, just a couple of lines to see what emerges out of it. Okay? Ready? Go...

Audience #1:	"Cumquat."
Audience #2:	"Would you please?"
Audience #1:	"Isn't this a nice restaurant."

Audience #2:   "(laughter) This is our third date."

Audience #1:   "You know, the funny thing about that is… I wasn't sure there would be a third date… and I figured, well if there's going to be a third date I'm just going to be who I am.

(Audience #2 gives Audience #1 a strange look)

(Audience laughter.)

Audience #2:   "Do you know that I could have been out with this other guy. But I thought you were nice. My mother recommended you."

Audience #1:   "Well, I never actually got to the third date with your mother. But…"

Audience #2:   (Gasp)

(Audience laughter.)

Audience #1:   "The cumquats she gave me in appreciation for the last time we were out… were sort of appropriate."

Audience #2:   "My mother has lived with my father for forty years. You screwed my mother."

Audience #1:   "Oh no… I got as far with her as I am with you right now."

(Audience laughter.)

"Now, I have more cumquats back at my place."

(Audience laughter)

And cut. Let's talk about this. We started with cumquat – a very simple concept and it became this whole thing about infidelity. The challenge here is to go beyond the word cumquat. I mean the literal word and make it take you to somewhere else. I think both of you did a great job listening to one another. That is an important element that must be present if the creative arc is to be achieved.

Sometimes in improvisation, the people working don't listen to one another. Instead, they just try to push through their own idea for the scene no matter what the other person is doing or saying. It makes it very difficult for the scene to progress when this happens. You want your improvisation, not matter how it starts, to be engaging to the participants and the audience alike. Now let's have two more volunteers.

> (Two new but reluctant audience members come up on the stage.)

Come on, you can do this.

> (A totally new person enters the room and comes up upon the stage.)

Okay, I'm going to set you up on this because you are coming in cold. We are going to give you a line – one of the audience is going to give you a line. This gentleman here has volunteered to give you a line.

> (Audience laughter.)

Now we want to give you a whole line (not just a word). So, think of something good. We will do two of these. The first, we will start with just one line and we will see what evolves. You may get up and move around if you want. Now for the audience here, let's bring it back home to where we started. We are writing and we have nothing more than a blank page in front of us.

> (Catalano is given the ten-minute signal.)

Ten minutes? Great. The first time we did this we put the word cumquat on a blank page, then we added to characters and we watched what evolved. Now, we are still on a blank page, we have two characters and in a moment one line. But we are not providing any of who, what, when or where. Visualize what is about to happen as a single line on a blank page. And now the line is?

> (Audience member: "I thought my turrets was cured.")

(Audience member on stage looking out at the suggested first line says "I'm going to kill you for this.")

(Audience laughter.)

Audience #1:	"I thought my turrets was cured."
Audience #2:	"I did too… but it sure isn't."
Audience #1:	"No, it isn't."
Audience #2:	"I guess you're mad."
Audience #1:	"I am… it comes out all the time."
Audience #2:	"You're really an embarrassment to the family."
Audience #1:	"Oh, well? I can handle that.
Audience #2:	"Why don't you get a handle on it?
Audience #1:	"It's just…"
Audience #2:	"No, it's weakness. You're just a weak person.
Audience #1:	"Well, it's really…"
Audience #2:	"You're just an embarrassment to the whole family. We are all successful and you sit around with this… this "
Audience #1:	"Well…"
Audience #2:	"It's not that… It's just like this, fuck, shit damn get out of my face.
Audience #1	"I can imagine that it would be an embarrassment to everybody, but I kind of like that."
Audience #2:	"You like it? You like embarrassing all of us? We all have doctorates and masters and you're going to embarrass the family."
Audience #1:	"Well, I have a doctorate but…"
Audience #2:	"Then why don't you go live in a cabin somewhere in the woods?"
Audience #1:	"Well, I'm looking for one."
Audience #2:	"Well, I hope you find one."
Audience #1:	"Okay, I will."
Audience #2:	"If you'll just go live there and stay away from the rest of the family and quit embarrassing us."
Audience #1:	"Okay."
Audience #2:	"Okay."

Okay, cut.

(Audience laughter.)

Okay, think of a line.

(Audience member "Did that improvisation have to be so mean?")

No, but it kind of went that way. But did you notice that the characters had a particular physicality and sound to them? Now for this next exercise we're going to think of a line and we're going to end it in that line. Let's call it "Last Line." We are just going to start cold and develop the "who, what, when and where," but as the scene progresses at some point (when it reaches a natural climax) we will end it with this line. The scene is not over until the last line is spoken within the context of the scene.

(Audience member asks: "Are we continuing the turrets scene?")

No, this is a totally new scene where we will create a totally new who, what, when and where. What I would like you to work on and think about is who you are and what is happening. Then as the scene comes to a natural conclusion, you will end it with this last line. We know it's over when the last line is spoken. So, if the last line given were "Merry Christmas," the improvisation is not over until that line is spoken.

(Audience member: "Does it matter who says the line?")

No.
Audience member: "So it's over whenever that line is spoken?"
Right.

(Audience member: "So, how do you get started?")

You just start with in this instance two characters in the room. Let me help you out a little bit. You're sitting in a waiting room for a job interview and the last line is? "So why is the lowest grade you got in ballroom dance?"

Audience #1:   "What are you waiting for?"

Audience #2:	"I'm interviewing for a part time position as an editor."
Audience #1:	"Oh, I'm interviewing for the full time as an editor."
Audience #2:	"Well, good. Then we're on different tracks."
Audience #1:	"I think there's only one position though…"
Audience #2:	"Do you think they made a mistake. I mean part time? Full time? You know?"
Audience #1:	"As far as I know there is only one position and if they can get somebody to work full time with part time pay."

(Audience laughter.)

Audience #1:	"They would rather have them… than a part time."
Audience #2:	"Well, we will just have to see. How did you get into this business?"
Audience #1:	"Went to school… then just did some writing… then some editing. What about you?"
Audience #2:	"Well, I just need some money. So I do whatever I can. I hope it's part time – I really don't want to work full time. Well, we will just have to see. But… what else to do you do?"
Audience #1:	"Well actually… I don't work at all. In fact, I just came into this room by accident. I'm a student.
Audience #2:	"College?"
Audience #1:	"You're probably thinking I'm way to old to go to college… but actually, I do very well. I have almost a 4.0 GPA."
Audience #2:	"Really? Why almost?"
Audience #1:	Well, all can't be good at everything. I got a "D" in ballroom dance…"
Audience #2:	"So why is the lowest grade you got in ballroom dance?"

And cut. Tune in next week to find out "why" her lowest grade was in ballroom dance. Perhaps she was doing a bit more than ballroom dancing with her partner Renaldo!"

Out of this scene, maybe two characters would evolve. Maybe they would become friends, leave the job interview go on an adventure. Maybe they decide to rob a bank or go on a spree… two women meet and want to change their boring lives. What do we have THELMA AND LOUISE (1991). And it all starts with two people meeting at a job interview and from that point the characters and the story evolve. Remember we started with a blank page and now we have three pages of dialogue. We may use very little of it or all of it... but we have now progressed off of the blank page to an idea. An idea that will evolve on it's own rather than be artificially crafted. We now have the beginning of our story and we have begun our journey on our feet!

I want to thank all of you for getting up here on this stage today. Let's all give one another a big round of applause for doing such a great job today!

Thank you very much and I hope you enjoy the rest of the conference. Thank you.

(Audience applause.)

www.ingramcontent.com/pod-product-compliance
Lightning Source LLC
Chambersburg PA
CBHW060949050426
42337CB00052B/3281